THE LITTLE
bOOK OF
EUROVISION

THE LITTLE
bOOK OF
EUROVISION

THE GLITZ, THE HITS,
AND THE RUSSIAN
GRANNIES

ALEXANDRA PARSONS

DOG 'n' BONE

Dedication
To all Eurovision contestants who scored nul points. BRAVO!

Published in 2022 by Dog 'n' Bone
An imprint of Ryland Peters & Small Ltd
20–21 Jockey's Fields   341 E 116th St
London WC1R 4BW   New York, NY 10029

www.rylandpeters.com

10 9 8 7 6 5 4 3 2 1

A CIP catalog record for this book is available from the Library of Congress and the British Library.

ISBN: 978-1-912983-51-3

Printed in China

Design concept: Geoff Borin
Designer: Louise Leffler
Illustrator: Blair Frame

Art director: Sally Powell
Production manager: Gordana Simakovic
Publishing manager: Penny Craig
Publisher: Cindy Richards

CONTENTS

BY WAY OF INTRODUCTION: SOME MEMORABLE MOMENTS

THE ONE WITH SPECTACULAR STAGING

In 2018, the Altice Arena in Lisbon was the venue for a spectacular opening act from Mélovin of Ukraine.
The song, with Halloween and vampires in mind, was "**Under the Ladder**." The art director, possibly determined to make a name for himself, devised a coffin/grand piano affair from which Mélovin emerged via a ladder which caught fire halfway through the song (just in case anyone was falling asleep). He got no votes from any professional jury apart from a few weaselly points from Azerbaijan and Moldova, but the popular vote propelled him into seventeenth place.

THE ONE WHEN THE SMOKE MACHINE WENT INTO OVERDRIVE

That would be 2015, in Vienna's Stadhalle, when Georgia's **Nina Sublatti**, instead of appearing in a mysterious veil of wispy vapor was engulfed in a thick cloud of black smoke. One of the pre-contest favorites, she came eleventh on the night.

THE ONE WITH THE DRUMMING GRANNY

It is 2005, the venue is Kiev's Palace of Sports in Ukraine. The Moldovian entry, "**Boonika Bate Doba**" (Grandma Beats the Drum), was performed by the group **Zdob și Zdub** which included their grandmother (or someone else's grandmother) sitting in a rocking chair beating a big bass drum. The much-treasured video to accompany this song featured a worldwide selection of drum-beating grannies. Powerful stuff.

WHY EUROVISION?

THE ORIGINAL AIMS
AND AMBITIONS AND HOW IT
GOT OUT OF HAND

The Eurovision Song Contest/*Concours Eurovision de la Chanson* started in 1956 as a simple simultaneous radio and television broadcast, dreamt up by Marcel Bezençon of the European Broadcasting Union (EBU) to test the limits of live transmission. But what a bedazzling, sequined monster it has become.

Lest we forget, 1956 was the year of the Suez crisis, and the Russian invasion of Hungary that cost over 2,000 lives. The setting for this song competition was a recently war-scarred Europe much in need of healing. It was also the year in which ideas of a common market and a united Europe were beginning to coalesce, and many of the institutions that were to further this aim were headed up by France, eager to be in pole position when it all kicked off and with an agenda to make French the language of Europe. The EBU took the even-handed decision to make both English and French its official languages, and that remains the case to this day. Presenters from host countries must smile and do

" **The setting for this song competition was a recently scarred Europe much in need of healing.** ,, what they do in both English and French: "Twelve points, *douze points.*"

The very first song competition/*concours de chanson* was held at the Teatro Kursaal in Lugano, Switzerland with seven participants: the Netherlands, Switzerland, Belgium, West Germany, France, Luxembourg, and Italy. The BBC, preoccupied with their own *Festival of British Popular Songs*, missed the deadline to register, as did the national broadcasters of Denmark and Austria, but all three did join in the jollity the following year. With so few participants in Lugano, each country was asked to enter two songs into the competition, and most of them hedged their bets with one jolly song and one lyric-driven *chanson*. Nothing too cutting edge, remember, for the early evening family audience.

The voting procedure was far less complicated than it is now. Each country sent two jurors to Lugano (apart from cash-strapped Luxembourg who had the Swiss jurors vote on their behalf). Votes were cast in secret, and each juror could vote for whoever they liked, including their own contestants. Needless to say, the Swiss won with **"Refrain,"** a simplistic wail of sadness and regret. You can catch the winner's reprise on YouTube should you need a dose of melancholia; the rest of the footage is sadly lost due to the carelessness of film storage facilities.

"You keep thinking this will make sense in a moment. But no."

Graham Norton, Portugal 2018

WHAT IS EUROPE?

You'd think you would know. Europe is bounded to the north and west by the Atlantic Ocean and its offshoots, and to the south by various seas such as the Mediterranean, Adriatic, and Aegean. To the east and northeast, boundaries become a bit fuzzy as the geographic border does not follow state boundaries. Traditionally, the Ural mountains and the Caspian sea have separated Europe from Asia, and to the Southeast it's the job of the Caucasus mountains and the Black Sea.

Anomalies occur. Iceland is in Europe, but neighboring Greenland, which is technically in North America, is owned by Denmark. Both Cyprus (which is in the EU) and Turkey (which is not) are geographically in Asia but politically inclined towards Europe and therefore regarded as transcontinental countries. Israel is technically in Asia but is regarded as European, just because it is European in outlook.

With all this confusion, it is hardly surprising that Eurovision's idea of what constitutes Europe shifts about at will, including both Morocco and Australia when it suits.

> " **Iceland is in Europe, but neighboring Greenland, which is technically in North America, is owned by Denmark.** "

THE MORE
THE MERRIER

The larger the audience, the greater the kudos for the EBU. It started with seven countries singing twice each to bulk up the show to a respectable one hour and 40 minutes. The following year, 10 countries took part, the show loosened up, the Netherlands won, and the Treaty of Rome was signed. More and more countries signed up as the years went by. More and more people had television sets. Europe became a Union. Some of the songs and performances were so ridiculous they gained cult followings. In the real world there was rock 'n' roll, reggae and soul, the Beatles, Jimi Hendrix, Bob Marley, The Who, and the Rolling Stones, but Eurovision ignored all that and ploughed its own furrow and the audience figures kept rising. The shows were now marathons, with participants from 50 plus countries strutting their stuff in semi-finals and finals over a whole week, and the audience figures kept rising.

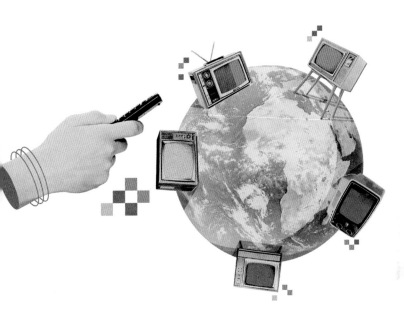

Opening and interval acts such as Cirque du Soleil, Riverdance, and Madonna grabbed even more attention, and the audience figures kept rising. In the UK we were lucky enough to enjoy the weary, acerbic commentaries of Terry Wogan and later Graham Norton, which added wicked wit to the experience of this surreal kitsch-fest, and the audience figures kept on rising.

In 2019 (the last Eurovision not compromised by *that* virus), 42 countries entered. As per the rules, the semi-finals whittled them down to 26. The final show on the Saturday lasted nearly four hours and 183 million people worldwide watched it live. Only YouTube knows how many more millions more streamed the event. It's the biggest TV audience for anything, ever. Marcel Bezençon died in 1981, the year that Bucks Fizz won for the UK, with the bouncy, optimistic "**Making Your Mind Up**" (prophetic or what?). One can only wonder what Monsieur Bezençon would think of his baby now.

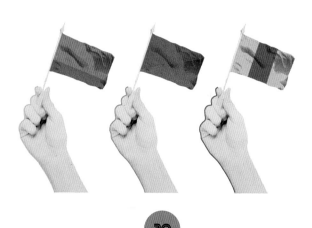

A PATTERN IS EMERGING

What did the 1956 competitors have in common apart from their enthusiasm for song contests? Well, they were all (apart from the host country Switzerland) members of the European Coal and Steel Community, one of the organizations, along with the European Atomic Energy Community, that formed the foundation stone of the European Common Market. A month after the competition those same countries met up to discuss forming a Customs Union.

And another thing, if you were to superimpose an 800AD map of Charlemagne's Holy Roman Empire when it was at its most powerful over a map of Europe in 1956, it would fit rather neatly over the borders of those first Eurovision participants.

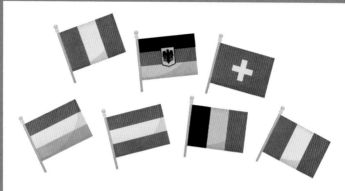

COLLECTOR'S ITEMS
THOSE FIRST
EUROVISION SONGS
IN NO PARTICULAR
ORDER

This is because, apart from the winner* (see page 25) the results of the voting were never published. You will notice that most of the songs were sung in French, in keeping with the whole France-being-top-country-in-Europe vibe.

FROM THE NETHERLANDS

UPLIFTING SONG NUMBER ONE:

"**De Vogels van Holland**" (The Birds of Holland)

Sung in Dutch, with maybe too many *toodle oodle oos*

in the chorus, by Jetty Paerl

SAD SONG NUMBER TWO:

"**Voorgoed Voorbij**" (Gone for Good)

Sung in Dutch by Corry Brokken

23

"Most countries hedged their bets with one jolly song and one lyric-driven *chanson*. Nothing too cutting edge. "

FROM SWITZERLAND

SONG NUMBER ONE WAS THE JOLLY ONE:
"**Das Alte Karussell**" (The Old Carousel)
Sung in German by Lys Assia

*SONG NUMBER TWO:
"**Refrain**" (as you would expect)
Sung in French, again by Lys Assia
(she was popular in the Alps)

FROM BELGIUM

SONG NUMBER ONE:
"**Messieurs les Noyés de la Seine**"
(Gentlemen Drowned in the Seine)
Sung in French, apparently quite reluctantly,
by Fud Leclerc

SONG NUMBER TWO:
"**Le Plus Beau Jour de Ma Vie**"
(The Best Day of My Life)
Sung in French by Mony Marc

25

FROM WEST GERMANY

SONG NUMBER ONE:
"Im Wartesaal zum Grossen Glück"
(In the Waiting Room for Good Luck)
Sung in German by Walter Andreas Schwarz

SONG NUMBER TWO:
"So Geht das Jede Nacht" (It's Like this Every Night)
Sung in German, with a bit of a nautical swing,
by Freddy Quinn

FROM FRANCE

SONG NUMBER ONE:
"Le Temps Perdu" (Wasted Time)
A chanson about lost love sung in French
by pretty blonde Mathé Altéry

SONG NUMBER TWO:
"Il Est Là" (He's There)
Another chanson about lost love sung in French by
pretty brunette Dany Dauberson

FROM LUXEMBOURG

SONG NUMBER ONE:
"**Ne Crois Pas**" (Don't You Believe It)
Sung in French by Michèle Arnaud

SONG NUMBER TWO:
"**Les Amants de Minuit**" (The Midnight Lovers)
Sung in French, again by Michèle Arnaud
(it was cheaper to send one singer)

FROM ITALY

SONG NUMBER ONE:
"**Aprite le Finestre**"
(Open the Windows)
An upbeat chanson about the arrival of spring,
sung in Italian by Franca Raimondi

SONG NUMBER TWO:
"**Amami Se Vuoi**"
(Love Me If You Want)
Sung in Italian by Tonina Torrielli who closed the show

EUROVISION 1956

BELGIUM	10	2	4	8			
FRANCE	6	10	1	3			
ITALY	3	4	10	7			
LUXEMBOURG	5	8	3		10		
NETHERLANDS	1	1	8				
SWITZERLAND	7	3	9				
WEST GERMANY	2	5	2				

+

3   1   4   8   10   5   2

2

VOTING
SYSTEMS AND
STRATEGIES

*I'll vote for you,
if you vote for me*

In the beginning (1956), jurors voted for their own countries—well who wouldn't? And no wonder the full scoring history of that initial contest has never been revealed. The organizers eventually woke up and realized that system was going nowhere. The following year there were new rules: jurors were not allowed to vote for their own country. Each country could appoint ten jurors, who could each award one vote for their favorite song and by this time there were ten participating countries. So that's a lot of judges, and a lot of points. Votes were relayed back to the venue by phone, so there's some joy to be had checking out black-and-white reportage of impeccably made-up female presenters on the phone, wrestling with bad connections, foreign jury spokespersons, adding up, maps with flags, and manual scoreboards.

TURNING UP
THE TENSION

It was not to last. Rules about voting changed
constantly in an effort to make the judging period less
boring for the viewers. Add a bit of tension! Watch
those scores accumulate! The ten-juror model worked
for a while, with people up on ladders in the studio
keeping a massive scoreboard up to date. As the list
of participants grew and grew, there came changes
in the number of points that could be awarded and
changes in the number of jurors. It was all getting
too much and then technology stepped in and made
televoting possible, so now 50 percent of the vote
is made up of votes from the general public, the
rest from "professional" jurors. A country's jury must
consist of five members from the music industry with
a mix of ages and genders, and the general populace
can vote by phone or text message or, of course, via
the official app.

WHO VOTES FOR WHOM?

Given that the top score one country can give to another is 12 points, here are some examples of totally unbiased mutual scoring:

Turkey and Azerbaijan are at the top of the pile, awarding each other the full 12 points every time they have voted.

Cyprus and Greece come next with 11.6 points. (There was a wobble… see When a Love Affair Goes Wrong, page 35.)

Moldovia and Romania have a pretty solid understanding, coming in at 11.5.

Bosnia-Herzegovina and Serbia keep each other happy
with an average of 10.5 points going each way.

IN OTHER NEWS:

★ Albania votes mostly for Italy, as does Malta.

★ Armenia, Belarus, Estonia, Latvia, and Ukraine vote overwhelmingly for Russia.

★ Austria and Croatia vote mostly for Serbia.

★ Belgium votes for the Netherlands and vice versa.

★ Denmark, Finland, and Norway vote for Sweden and Sweden votes for them in return.

★ France votes for Turkey a lot, and so does Germany—this can partly be explained by the Turkish diaspora, who are obviously keen Eurovisioners, and presumably all of them have downloaded the app.

★ Georgia votes for neighboring Armenia.

★ Hungary spreads its bets, but it's mostly Netherlands and Iceland.

★ Iceland tends to vote for Denmark.

★ Ireland likes Lithuania and Latvia, but they have given the UK a few points in the past.

WHEN A LOVE AFFAIR GOES WRONG

Greece and Cyprus, voting buddies since way back, had a big falling out in 2015 when the Cypriot jury (not the people) marked the Greek entry down despite the singer, Maria Elena Kyriakou coming from the island. It wasn't as if she stood a chance of winning, as that year the top two places were a close-run thing between Russia and Sweden, but it did cause a major upset, so major that the affair was discussed at some length in the parliaments of both Greece and Cyprus. As if they didn't have anything better to do.

- ★ Israel favors Russia and Ukraine.
- ★ Italy favors Ukraine and Moldova.
- ★ Lithuania votes for Latvia.
- ★ Macedonia votes massively for Albania, but Albania doesn't return the favor.
- ★ The Netherlands vote for Turkey (see diaspora above) and also Belgium.
- ★ Poland votes mostly for Ukraine, but they also show a bit of love for Belgium.
- ★ Portugal votes for Spain (and Moldova).
- ★ Russia favors Azerbaijan and Armenia.
- ★ Slovenia votes for Serbia, as does Switzerland.
- ★ Spain favors Romania and Italy.
- ★ The UK is pretty much even-handed, but gives most points to Ireland, followed by Greece.

What we learn from all this is that nobody, apart from a few grudging points from Ireland and Malta, is particularly keen to vote for the UK, even if they come up with a cracking song.

MAKING A WEEK OF IT: SEMI-FINALS AND FINALS

By 1993, so many Eastern Bloc countries in Europe were signing up for the glitterfest, that a weeding-out process was implemented. The preselection involved seven countries from Central and Eastern Europe, and it was held a month before the main event. Two countries made it through, and the others had to skip a year before they could apply, and the seven lowest scoring nations also had to skip a year. This crazy shuffle system carried on for several years until someone had the bright idea to introduce semi-finals! As no one wanted to upset the influential nations who had been there from the beginning (or the guardians of the EBU's purse strings), Germany, France, Spain, the UK, and Italy (known as the Big Five) automatically qualify for the final in perpetuity (or until another rule change), along with the host country and the top ten scoring countries from the previous year. Do keep up. The top ten semi-finalists join the Five, the host country and the ten who impressed the previous year to make a total of 26 finalists. Twenty-six! That's a lot of **** to sit through. Which is why you will find recommendations for some awesomely lethal cocktails in the Watch Party section (see pages 138-140).

For some, the joy of the semi-finals is that there are two of them! Held in the week before the grand final on the Saturday, it means dedicated Eurovisioners can mainline with a triple dose of **La la la! Ding dong ding! Boom-bang-a-bang!** and that all-time classic **Wham-bam-boom!**

———————

"In the last few years, the semi-finals have weeded out some of the Eurovision lunacy... but not this year"

Graham Norton

———————

WHY WIN?

To the victor the crown! Yay! But quite an uncomfortable crown to wear. The winning country hosts the next year's contest. That does give the host nation a chance to wheel out a whole lot of Tourist Board info, and yes, there will be a worldwide audience for the picture the host nation wishes to paint, but at what cost? This circus is becoming increasingly expensive, and for not that much in the way of payback. The EBU hands over about €6 million in registration fees, and then there's the fans crowding into the venue, buying tickets, staying in hotels, and mainlining Babycham, but that's a drop in the bucket. The average show costs about €25 million— that would be a $30 million/£22 million bucket.

VOTING SYSTEMS & STRATEGIES

FANS AND SUPERFANS

183 MILLION AND RISING

"**It's fun to be a fan! There's even talk of a three-day cruise! Can't wait.**"

Fasten your seatbelts, you are entering the world of superfandom. There is a network of 46 registered Eurovision fan club sites under the umbrella of the General Organization of Eurovision Fans/*Organisation Générale des Amateurs de l'Eurovision*. Or OGAE as those of us in the know call it. It was founded in 1984 in Finland, where the winter nights are very long, encouraging people to stay home and obsess. The HQ of OGAE is in Savonlinna, Finland, and it has a website should you wish to know more. Any country that has participated is eligible to register a fan club, which is as it should be. However, such is the extraordinary reach of Eurovision that in addition to the registered clubs, there are a further 39 countries that have "Rest of the World" (RoW) affiliated status. That is a humongous number of people. You will find enthusiastic OGAE RoW clubs in countries as surprising as Brazil, Egypt, Japan, Namibia, China, South Korea, and the United Arab Emirates to name but a few.

The clubs are very active: apart from scrunching statistics they are kept busy issuing videos of every song ever sung and publishing every lyric in its original language as well as in English. They run pre-Eurovision contests amongst themselves to see who can spot the winners and they hold run-offs for the losers—the Second Chance Contest. It's massive. Do the math: 65 years of competition multiplied by an average of 40 songs a year, then add in the rejects from the national competitions which also figure. So THOUSANDS of songs, that should be best forgotten, have been lovingly played over and over, archived and analyzed by an army of people who probably look quite normal.

It's fun to be a fan! If you are lucky, your local branch will run monthly karaoke parties and quiz nights, hold meetings in church halls to discuss and analyze the national competitions, and organize Watch Parties when the real thing comes along. They may also be able to score tickets for the live show. There's even talk of a three-day cruise! Can't wait.

Eurovision host:
"There's so much love in the room tonight!"
Graham Norton:
"Not for you."

"Eurovision knows a thing or two about psychology. "

SUCKING THEM IN

Eurovision knows a thing or two about psychology. *"Extraordinary how potent cheap music is,"* observed Noel Coward, and there you have Eurovision in a nutshell. They also know how to stoke up the fans. There's a competition on the official website for fans to send in videos of themselves singing, dancing, and dressing up to perform their favorite Eurosongs. They are loaded up to YouTube for online broadcast. Obviously, there are terms and conditions, and somewhere in there permissions will have been sought and granted, but imagine the shame! Imagine if someone, somewhere digs up evidence of you dressed as a canary performing "**Sing Little Birdie**."

WHAT ELSE?

Of course, there's a podcast: "Bringing you the guests, games, and glitter from the world of Eurovision!", and you can tune in every Wednesday. And there's *Eurovoix* news, which brings you up to date daily on who is being considered for what, discussion on the host city, news about presenters, news about the jurors, stories about participants in Junior Eurovision and much, much more. You can live and breathe Eurovision every day of the week, should you wish. People tweet about it until there's nothing left to say and then they tweet some more. There are fans on many a private Facebook page, keeping each other up to date with glitter news and statistics. There are several sites run by devoted fans who have researched, transcribed, and translated every lyric to every song ever sung on the Eurovision stage, and there have been well over 1,500 such magic moments…

Let us not forget the merchandise. The well-dressed Eurovisioner can purchase T-shirts, hats, hoodies, socks, necklaces, and country-specific scarves. They can stuff their stuff into a tote bag or a gym bag, adding a logoed water bottle for credibility. For the home there are posters, mugs, trophies, and memorial zero-euro notes. And for the music library? Don't ask.

LGBTQ COMMUNITY

A big fan base here and with all that gloriously camp glitter and glitz, who would be surprised? And guess who hosts the best Watch Parties? The contest organizers realized what a huge hit they had on their hands with the gay community when Paul Oscar, an openly gay singer, did his bit for diversity and Iceland in 1997 and the following year Dana International, the first trans performer to appear on the Eurovision stage, won for Israel with the anthemic "**Diva**." Since then, we've enjoyed the rousing vocals of glamorous drag queen Conchita Wurst who won for Austria in 2014, and bisexual Duncan Laurence winning for the Netherlands in 2019, and there have been performers in the past who have openly celebrated same sex relationships both male and female in song and dance, often with a kiss. Of course, diversity doesn't go down well everywhere. Both Hungary and China

terminated broadcasting rights in protest, and when
Russia outlawed "gay propaganda" in 2013 they
discovered the hard way that it was best not to upset
the Eurovision "family." Their 2014 contestants, the
Tolmachevy Sisters, were roundly booed, poor things.
The following year, the organizers, expecting further
protests, installed anti-booing technology, so the TV
audience were boo-free, but the Russian contestant,
Polina Gagarina, could hear the boos from the
dressing room and sobbed throughout the contest.
But she came second so that cheered her up!

A THOUGHTFUL MOMENT

Eurovision is a drug. Once sucked in, there are tentacles everywhere to keep you hooked into feeling part of a family, albeit a tin-eared family on the run from the Taste Police. So, to the many fans, contentedly soaking up the nice warm feeling that comes from being immersed in an event that claims, quite simply, that it was "created to unite a continent"—what can you say? Let it be.

" ... you are hooked into feeling part of a family, albeit a tin-eared family on the run from the Taste Police. "

BEING THERE

For the true fan, nothing beats being there. After the parties, it's the next step in the addiction cycle. Fans say it is something to do with spreading peace by reducing rivalries to a *Ja Ja Ding Dong*. Of course it's nice to be among people who think the same as you, of course it is.

Tickets are available either from your local OGAE club which gets you into the fanzone by the stage, or from the official website. The truly obsessed can get tickets for all six rehearsals and all three live shows. Can you have too much of a good thing? Anyway, you would have to save up. Tickets can cost up to 180 euros for a semi-final rehearsal, and over 400 euros for the Grand Final live show.

FANS & SUPERFANS

THE SONGS,, THE SONGS!

WHO COMMISSIONS THEM?
WHO WRITES THEM?
WHO CARES?

"**...some countries have a deep pool of song-writing talent and others have a puddle**"

bO

Some people do care, but not that much. It's quite rare to get a serious talent involved in this kitsch-fest, partly because it is deeply uncool and partly because the European Broadcasting Union want a level playing field and while some countries have a deep pool of songwriting talent, others have a puddle. But someone's got to do it, and that someone would be the people who signed up to the EBU ideal: the broadcasters.

In general, national TV stations in the various countries encourage songwriters to submit their work. The duds are whittled out, leaving the best of the bunch in competition. Selected artists are invited to perform the chosen songs in a televised competition and the viewing public then have a say in the choosing the winning song and performer—so there is definitely an element of the entire population of a country being open to blame for the outcome.

THE SONG-WRITING RULES

There are some rules. In fact, there are lots of rules and they keep changing, but this is where things stand right now. The song must be an original composition and the composer/songwriter can't hedge bets with multiple entries as only one submission is allowed. It must be a song that hasn't been publicly released or performed in public, although these days streaming sites make a mockery of that. It's got to be a song with lyrics, and somebody has to sing them, so it is as well to compose a tune that does not require perfect pitch and an operatic level of breath control. If a group, it is limited to six members. All performers must be over 18. Mercifully, the song can't be longer than three minutes, and the act cannot include live animals. These days the powers that be are quite strict about rude lyrics and political rants.

The competing songs are generally submitted as video clips, so no need to learn to read or write music. If chosen, the songwriter may or may not get a bit of help with the technical side of things. Back in the day a full orchestra was provided by the host nation, but it proved to be too expensive, and quite frankly not a gig any self-respecting musician would sign up for. From 1999 onward, the music has been on pre-recorded backing tapes. But vocals must be live, so no hiding place there.

"OK... That's three minutes we'll never get back, but look at it this way: we'll never have to hear that song again."

Graham Norton referring to Albania's 2015 entry

THERE HAVE BEEN HITS!

Not all Eurovision songs are just rubbish. Some of them have become quite popular rubbish.

1976

The 1976 winning song for the UK's Brotherhood of Man, **"Save Your Kisses for Me,"** sold over six million copies. Composed by two members of the band, the song is bouncy and trite, but saved by the revelation in the last line that it is being sung to a three-year-old kid, so trite/cute. Sailing very close to plagiarism though: try listening to "Tie a Yellow Ribbon Round the Old Oak Tree" and see what you think.

1958

"**Nel Blu, Dipinto del Blu**," performed and co-composed by singer/songwriter Domenico Modugno came third for Italy in 1958. Once translated into English and renamed "**Volare**," the song was recorded by artists as diverse as Dean Martin, Ella Fitzgerald, David Bowie, and Frank Zappa. "Volare" achieved combined sales of over 22 million copies worldwide, was voted the second greatest Eurovision song ever, and scored two Grammy awards. Why didn't it win? Ask the Eurovision judges. The winner that year was a dreary French ballad-y lullaby "**Dors, Mon Amour**." Sales figures for this song are impossible to unearth.

1967

Swinging London, and all eyes were on British design, fashion, and music. Up popped mini-skirted, bare-footed Sandie Shaw with "**Puppet on a String**" written by Bill Martin and Phil Coulter. This is Sandie's take on the song that became a worldwide smash and sold over four million copies: *"I hated it from the very first oompah to the final bang on the big bass drum. I was instinctively repeled by its sexist drivel and cuckoo-clock tune."*

1968

The following year, Bill Martin and Phil Coulter tried to repeat the winning formula for the UK with "**Congratulations**," and persuaded a youthful Cliff Richard to take it to Europe. Close but no cigar. He was pipped to first place by the Spanish entry, "**La La La**." However, "Congratulations" became a worldwide hit, while "La La La" disappeared without trace.

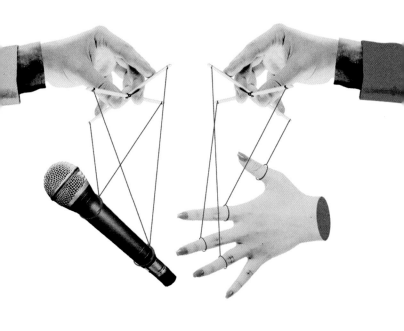

THE SONGS, THE SONGS!

1974

In 1974 Abba changed the face of Europop by winning the contest with "**Waterloo**." The single was number one practically everywhere, reached the top 10 in the USA, sold upward of six million copies, and was voted the best Eurovision song of all time. Since then, well… Mamma Mia!

THE SONGS, THE SONGS!

THE SONG THAT TRIGGERED A COUP D'ETAT

In 1974, Portugal was on the brink of revolution. Plans were laid, and groups of patriotic conspirators gathered in key locations awaiting the signal to revolt. And the signal, broadcast on April 24th at 10.55 pm, was none other than Portugal's entry in the Eurovision Song Contest that had taken place a couple of weeks earlier. **"E Depois do Adeus"** (After Goodbye) signaled the start of something new. By the end of the following day, with overwhelming support from the people, Portugal had a new democratic government. A very Eurovision way of bringing about change with a song. Tra la.

1997

Katrina and the Waves, an Anglo-American band, won a decisive victory for the UK in 1997 with "**Love Shine a Light**." The song was written by band member Kimberley Rew to celebrate the thirtieth anniversary of the Swindon branch of the suicide prevention charity, The Samaritans. Not just a warm fuzzy feeling, its anthemic status made it a slow-burn hit.

1981

The UK'S Bucks Fizz won in 1981 with the bouncy, new-decade optimism of "**Making Your Mind Up**," which was written specifically as a Eurovision entry by songwriter Andy Hill. The group was hastily assembled for the competition. Even before the contest, the song reached the British charts, featured on BBC TV's *Top of the Pops*, and scored the group an album deal. Their actual live performance on the night was not their best. Off-key some say, but they won, nonetheless. The song hit number one in many countries and sold over four million copies. Here's a thing: the BBC made a promotional video of the group wandering aimlessly around Harrod's department store. Needless to say, all future promotions used footage of the group's appearance on *Top of the Pops*.

2012

In 2012, the contest was held in Azerbaijan, a country that comes 140th out of 167 in The Economist Magazine's Democracy Index. The Swedish winner was the upbeat and positive "**Euphoria**," sung by Loreen and written by Thomas Gustafsson. "Euphoria" soared above the competition. In second place were Buranovskiye Babushki, six grandmothers from a village 1,000 kilometers east of Moscow (still in Europe by a whisker) singing in Udmurt, a language not many people speak. The Russian Grannies got to 159 in the British charts, "Euphoria," on the other hand, sold millions and is the most downloaded Eurovision song to date.

2014

It is 2014 and we are in Denmark. The Russians are sulking, the Ukrainians on the edge of civil war, and along comes Eurovision to pour balm on the waters. The Austrian entry is "**Rise Like a Phoenix**," a song composed by Ali Zuckowski that every major record label in Austria had refused to produce. Perfect for Eurovision, reasoned Zuckowski. The song was performed with panache by Conchita Wurst, a character created by actor/singer Tom Neuwirth. Conchita came out on stage bearded, beautiful, and glittery. The audience not surprisingly expected yet another Austrian novelty song. But they were wrong, Conchita was a fine singer with a strong voice, performing an anthem of hope. Juries and televoters unanimously gave her first place. The Russian contingent proclaimed that Eurovision had become *"a hotbed of sodomy at the initiation of European liberals"* and urged Russia to boycott the competition. That didn't happen. Conchita is in demand all over the world as a performer and gay pride icon, and Zuckowski's song just keeps on streaming.

1980

Johnny Logan won for Ireland in 1980 with "**What's Another Year**," written by Irish songwriter and television presenter, Shay Healy. It got to number one in the UK, Irish, and several other European charts. Voted third best Eurovision song ever, it earned Shay Healy over a quarter of a million pounds in royalties. The winning theme? A tender song about waiting for someone who doesn't love you to come round to the idea of loving you.

2019

In 2019, against a backdrop of Israeli/Palestinian conflict, "**Arcade**," written and sung by Duncan Lawrence of the Netherlands, was the low-key winner. No pyrotechnics, no politics, he just sat at a piano and sang his song. It made the Billboard Hot 100 in the US and has been streamed over one billion times.

1996

"**Ooh Aah... Just a Little Bit**," written by Simon Caldwell and Steve Rodway and performed by Gina G, came eighth in 1996 for the UK. It sold nearly 800,000 records, and got to number one in the UK singles chart and number 12 on the Billboard Hot 100. The vibe was techno and the lyrics a bit double-entendre. The winner was "**The Voice**" written by Brendan Graham and performed for Ireland by Eimear Quinn. "The Voice" didn't trouble the British or US charts but got to number three in Ireland and number 21 in the Netherlands. Why did it win? It was a timely song about transcending pain and getting together to find peace, so 12 points all round.

5

LANGUAGES AND LYRICS

Do any of the words make sense?

As the contest groped its way toward superstardom there were, as you would expect, many changes to the rules about the language of the lyrics. At first there were no restrictions, but as the countries taking part were fairly mainstream and they stuck to their own languages, that was okay for a bit. Then Baltic states joined in, and then a cluster of Nordic countries, and while adding to the fun and bewilderment for all, it gave rise to bloc voting tactics, with neighboring countries voting for each other, probably because they were the only people who could vaguely understand what was being sung about, but more likely because they didn't want Old Europe to win at anything. The EBU kept changing their minds about language rules, because obviously a song in English stood a better chance of (a) being understood and (b) selling a few copies. They finally saw sense in 1999. But songwriters are a perverse lot, and with total freedom came the opportunity to mess around with different languages and even pluck one from their imagination. Take Belgian composer Michel Vangheluwe, who came up with "*O julissi na jalyni, O julissi na dytini, O bulo diti non slukati, Sestrone dina katsu….*" Which he claimed reminded him of his childhood. Belgium crashed out in the 2008 semi-finals with that one.

"They've got four languages in Belgium, and they're singing in an imaginary one. The very essence of Eurovision."

Terry Wogan

SOME OF
THE BEST

It will come as no surprise that there is a contest and a prize-giving structure for the best lyrics. It's called the **Eurostory Best Lyrics Award**. The shortlist is drawn up by a "small committee of poets that publish in the Dutch language." Wouldn't you just love to be a fly on the wall? The winner is chosen by an international jury of poets, writers, songwriters, and artists. They are looking for striking metaphors, strong lines, and poetic images. First off, they awarded prizes for the best line. Here are some recent winners:

2016

WINNER
The winning line came from Jamala, from Ukraine.
Her plaintive cry for freedom, "**1944**,"
also won Eurovision that year:
You think you are gods, but everyone dies.

In second place was the song from San Marino:
*I didn't know that you wished for the moon
to provide me light.*

Third place belonged to Hungary with:
*You feel mistreated in a world where the
poems sound fake.*
Couldn't agree more.

2017

WINNER
Nazim Khaled of France won with this
enigmatic thought:
*Centuries appear and disappear, that which you thought
was death, is a season, and nothing more than that.*

In second place came Norway's Joakim with:
I'm coping with a map that is roadless.

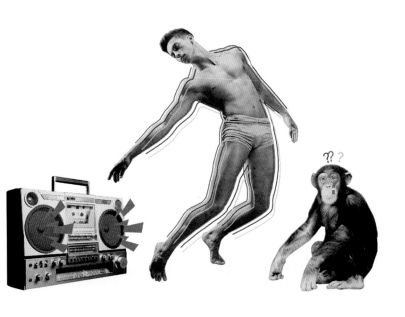

Third was a song from Italy which credits
no less than four songwriters. They came up
with this cracker of a line:
Evolution stumbles but the naked monkey dances.

2018

WINNER
Madame Monsieur won for France with this line
from their song "**Mercy**."
I am all those children who were taken by the sea:
I'll live a hundred thousand years.
To give them a break, it does sound better in French:
Je suis tous ces enfants que la mer a pris
Je vivrai cent mille ans, je m'appelle Mercy

Second was Switzerland for the snappy line:
We're the liars in the face of facts:
different weapon but the same attack.

Third place went to the Czech Republic's
Mikolas Josef for this:
Honey bunny up all night wannabe
couple goals queen
I know you "bop-whop-a-lu bop"
on his wood bamboo when
You were still seeing me and
well he didn't even knew
What had the poets been up to the night before
they awarded that prize?

2019

WINNER

This was the year the judges fell for an entire song,
"Soldi" (Money) by Mahmood.
The song was praised as a painful and beautiful song
about a boy, his cheating father, and his loving, abandoned
mamma…. "There are cinematic sentences," gushed the
judges, "that could have come straight out of a short story."

You haven't told yet what you had to tell
Betrayal is a bullet in the chest
Keep all your mercy to yourself
You keep lying at home but you know that she knows.
And so on.

Runners up were Czech Republic with another raunchy song
about sex with someone other than your current partner.
Here's a taster:

Can you hear it?
There's someone behind the wall making the same sounds
Can you hear it?

It sounds like you and me when we're making love
Who is it?
You said you wish they weren't taking such a long time.

2021

WINNER
First place for the best song lyrics goes to Italy, again.
The group Måneskin wrote and performed
"Zitti e Buoni" (Be Quiet and Behave).
The jury considered it "a raw cry from the misfits
of this fake society." Here's a sample:
These machine-men not climbing the rapids
I've written on a tombstone, in my house there's no God
But if you find the sense of time you'll climb out of your oblivion
And there's no wind stopping the natural power.

SOME OF THE WORST

For Austria in 2012, the hip-hop duo Trackshittaz came up with "**Woki Mit Deim Popo**" which translates as "**Shake Your Ass**." As you visualize this performance, include backing dancers in neon green spandex:
Your bum has feelings, your bum is a part of you,
Don't put it on chairs, your bum has an opinion, yeah.

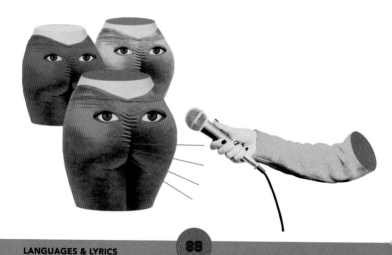

In the same year, passionate European Rambo Amadeus sang "**Euro Neuro**" for Montenegro. Who is Rambo? Well, he describes himself as "one of the most prominent cult figures on the ex-Yugoslav music scene." Here is a sample of his sophisticated approach to song-writing that so impressed the judges:

I got only one rule
Always stay cool
Like a swimming pool

Banal lines win prizes! Albeit a prize for the worst lines ever written. We go back to 1975 for this beauty, when the Dutch band Teach-In won the contest with "**Ding-A-Dong**." This song got to number one in the Swiss and Norwegian charts.

Try to sing a song that goes ding-ding-a-dong
There will be no sorrow when you sing tomorrow
And you walk along with your ding-ding-dong.

89

Here another contender from Norway's Alexander Rybak. **"That's How You Write A Song"** came fifteenth in 2018.

Sing shoobie doobie dat dat (shoobie doobie dat dat)
Shaba daba hey (shaba daba hey)
Say all day long (all day long)
And that's how you write a song.

Time now for some thoughtful philosophising on the human condition. Alf Poier romped into 6th place for Austria in 2003 with **"Weil Der Mensch Zählt"** (Man is the Measure of All Things):

The difference between people
Between apes and primates
It—it's not much bigger
Than between noodles and pancake strips.

Ireland trying to be ironic and knowing here, hoping the judges will be charmed by the insider track on the contest: Yes, it's Dustin the Turkey, who didn't make it past the semi-finals in 2008 with **"Irlande Douze Points."** Dustin was the turkey/vulture cross television presenter character created by comedian John Morrison. A sample of the lyrics sung by a turkey in English with a heavy Dublin accent:

Drag acts and bad acts and Terry Wogan's wig
Mad acts and sad acts, it was Johnny Logan's gig
Block votes! Shock votes! Give us your 12 today.

Saving the best for last: Russia's ethnic pop band Buranovskiye Babushki (Grannies from Buranovo.) The six elderly women sang **"Party For Everybody"** in the 2012 contest, and they came second—well done! They sang this merry song in Urdmut and English:

The cat is happy, the dog is happy,
The cat is happy, the dog is happy,
We are in a wonderful mood and very happy,
We are in a wonderful mood, oh joy.
There is more…

If there were a contest for the world's least catchy song title, there are some serious contenders from the selection shows. From Estonia in 2013 the punk metal band Winny Puhh came up with: **"A Local Man Korsakov Went To Latvia Yesterday,"** and from the same inspired bunch in 2006: **"Noodles And Sour Milk**." The winner, however, has to be the Buranovo Grannies' entry in the Russia's Eurovision Song Selection show in 2010. They mercifully did not win with **"Dlinntoniaja-dlinnaja Beresta I Kak Sdelat' Iz Nee Ajšon"** (*Very Long Birch Bark and How to Turn It into a Turban*)

LA LA LA, NOT LA L'A LA

In 1968, social order in France was being challenged by cobble-throwing students, Czechoslovakia was invaded, and Northern Ireland was deeply troubled. In this year of Euro-upheaval, Spain put forward a song in Catalan by Ramón Arcusa and Manuel de la Calva. The chosen performer was to be Joan Manuel Serrat, a Catalan man with a mission. However, Spanish dictator Franco insisted that the song be sung in Castilian, or proper Spanish as he would have it. Serrat refused to go along with that diktat and 21-year-old pop singer Massiel stepped up at the last minute to sing "**La La La**." But the la la las were in Castilian not Catalan so that was okay. AND SHE WON! Beating Cliff Richard and "**Congratulations**" by one point, *un point*. To be fair, it wasn't all la la la, there were some other words in the verses.

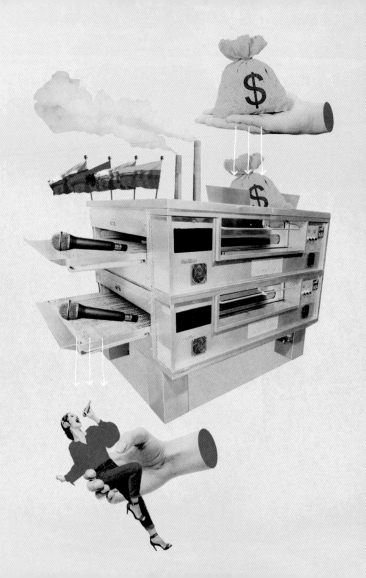

THE CONTESTANTS! THE OUTFITS!

Making an impact

There are rules, of course, about who is allowed up on that stage. Contestants must be consenting adults in their right minds, and no performer can sing for two different countries in the same show… so far that makes sense. However, there is nothing in the rule book about the nationality of the performer, meaning that a nation can ask pretty much whoever they like to perform on their behalf. This was good news for small countries like Luxembourg, Andorra, San Marino, and Monaco who didn't have much in the way of a local talent pool, but in the end, many of them didn't have the will or the funds to keep up with the big hitters or the former Soviet Bloc countries whose governments poured money into the contest in order to prove a point.

"He's always got his Hotel Management degree. I feel he's going to use it."

Graham Norton on Hungary's 2016 entrant

THE LITTLE COUNTRIES

Tiny Luxembourg was an enthusiastic competitor from the beginning up until 1994, when they were relegated and subsequently gave up trying. But back in the day they won the contest five times, which is a lot more than most. None of the winning performers were Luxembourgish—four were French and one was Greek. And of course, with a win, comes the burden of hosting the contest the following year. It all got too much. Andorra hasn't had much luck with talent, never having made it to the grand final. Their best shot was with the Danish singer **Susanne Georgi** in 2009, who almost qualified in a semi-final. Monaco was also enthusiastic at the beginning, but when they won in 1971 thanks to French singer **Séverine** (who unadvisedly declared she had never set foot in Monaco) they had to look to France to bail them out of hosting the following year.

San Marino, with only 33,500 inhabitants do have one singer to boast about, **Valentina Monetta**, who has represented the country four times, their other entries were mostly performed by **Senhit**, who is Italian but lives nearby. Neither singer ever made it to the grand final.

BIG AMBITIONS

Technically, it would be permissible to get Beyoncé or Taylor Swift or Ed Sheeran to roll up and sing for their favorite holiday destination, but it probably wouldn't happen. Talented performers who can sing are very unlikely to want to be associated with Eurovision. Most of the contestants who were or turned out to be big names, like **Abba**, **Cliff Richard**, **Julio Iglesias**, **Lulu**, **Olivia Newton-John**, and **Celine Dion** were caught unawares at the beginning of their careers. But that in a way is all part of the joy of Eurovision and its gloriously amateur enthusiasm. Eurovision is no longer a launch-pad to a

career, it's more of a fun day out for people with day jobs to go back to, and a safety net for catching the washed-up on their way down. There is a list of winners in the back of the book (see pages 142–143); run your eyes down it and ask yourself who *are* these guys?

WHAT TO WEAR?

There have been some outfits. For the more obscure countries there's a temptation to go heavy on cultural values and take the folkloric national costume route. However, countries with more confidence have come up with some eye-wateringly bizarre outfits over the years, possibly to distract from what our ears have to suffer. The idea that an outfit could help win the competition probably

came from the moment when the girls in **Bucks Fizz**, at the climax of the song, had their modest skirts ripped off by the boys to reveal tiny miniskirts. That was way back in 1981 when sexual stereotyping was seen as quite normal. Anyway, it was a winning move, and it has since encouraged others.

There is, of course a competition for outfits run by the fans. It's the **Barbara Dex Award** named after the Belgian singer who pitched up to the 1993 contest wearing a home-made, beige, semi-transparent, shapeless shroud that made her look like a badly wrapped-up parcel. Since then, there have been too many stripes, too much green velvet, too-busy patchwork, and many other *faux pas* to horrify the fashionistas. Now the focus has shifted, and the award is given to the "most striking look," of which there are many, and in so many categories of weird that it is hard to know where to begin.

In no particular order then, these are the contenders for our own Excess in Dress Awards:

Who could forget heavy metal Finnish band **Lordi**, who won the contest in 2006 with "**Hard Rock Hallelujah**?" It's hard to describe the look. It was heavy metal all right, with a mix of prosthetic devil/corpse masks, fur, chains, bad teeth, studs, and claws, a lot of black leather, some horns, and many dead flowers.

Mention must be made of Moldova. In 2013 **Aliona Moon** sang "**O Mie**" with passion. Her five-meter-long dress, with its white bodice and red skirt, became a canvas for some nifty front projection that got more heated as the song progressed. A cunning circular platform, concealed beneath her skirt, rose up at the climax of the song to reveal the full length of her dress and images of consuming flames. Top that.

★ ★ ★

"**Fallen Angel**" was a winner for Norway costume-wise,
but the song only made it to number 18 out of 26. **Tix**,
aka Andreas Haukeland, was dressed up like a winged
swan/angel in a floor-swishing white coat of feathers and
sequins. There were chains, there was a gold lamé body
suit, sunglasses, and a cast of horned devil dancers.
Fabulous, darling.

★ ★ ★

103 THE CONTESTANTS! THE OUTFITS!

Drag *artiste* **Verka Serduchka**, a comically vulgar railway sleeping car attendant character created by Andriy Danylko, put on a good show for Ukraine in 2007 with **"Dancing Lasha Tumbai."** She wore a metallic trench coat and a disco-ball hat, while the backing dancers looked like Boy Scouts wrapped in tin foil with pointy hats. Oh, and a lot of sequins.

★ ★ ★

As alter-egos go, **Dustin the Turkey** is perhaps the most baffling of characters to enter a singing competition. The year was 2008. The song, for Ireland, had too many words and the outfits on stage had too much going on. Dustin sat at a keyboard hidden by festoons of stuff wearing a turkey/vulture headdress that must have made it hard to project (see page 91.) The Turkey wore a gold lamé jacket with epaulettes, and the backing singers were in tight lamé dresses, with feathers, and there were loincloths.

★ ★ ★

No one did folkloric better than the grannies from Buranova who, among all the sequined glitter and raunchy pop, took to the Eurovision stage in 2012 wearing their traditional Urdmut outfits and singing a song about children coming home to a family party. Their comfortably loose dresses, in vibrant shades of red, were decorated with embroidered motifs that date back centuries. The impact came from there being six of them, all slightly different, but all reassuringly peasanty with that well-worn, lived-in look. Made everyone smile.

Special mention: not a contestant, but a male model in a parade at the start of the 2016 contest hosted by Sweden. He's in salmon pink tights and his upper half is a tiered wedding cake of white ruffs.

"Her outfit does involve some roadkill. I fear some Georgian crows were harmed in the making of this act."

Graham Norton on Georgia's 2015 entry

TROPHIES!

What's in it for the winner? Basically, a bunch of flowers, a trophy for the bookshelf, and a chance to wow the world with a reprise of their winning song. In the beginning there were a variety of silver cups, then someone had the idea of something arty in glass, but finally in 2008 the trophy was standardized. The permanent official trophy is now a handmade crystal rendition of an old-fashioned microphone, sandblasted and painted and, for Eurovision, quite restrained. It was designed by Swedish glass artist Kjell Engman. The winning lyricists and composers are not left out: they get smaller versions. You can buy mini replicas to award yourself from the official Eurovision shop, they only cost €250 ($295, or £215) and they weigh 2kg (4½lb), so that's a lot of glass for a lot of money.

7

HOSTS,
PRESENTERS, AND
COMMENTATORS

CRAMMING STARDUST INTO
A PAPER BAG

Each host nation must find from one to four hosts who can carry off the grueling job of presenting from the venue with grace and enthusiasm. They must take the live audience and the TV audience with them on a very long rollercoaster ride with quite a lot of dreary bits, and they have to look alert and interested while doing it. Not an easy job.

The worst bit to get through is the voting. This is a long and boring part of the show, but a winner must be found on the night, so it's got to be done.

During the actual televoting, there will be an interval act, or two. It's not unknown to have some stonking performance from a global superstar that does little for the self-confidence of the contestants, who are by now gathered together in the Green Room, necking the free champagne, gushing about how wonderful it was there up on stage, and practicing their losing-with-grace smiles as they await their ranking.

Next comes The Announcing and Counting of the Votes. This is a showcase for an advanced form of Cloud infrastructure, apparently. The phrase "digital engagement" is used a lot—if that helps. What it means on the ground is that there's a live link to each country's spokesperson who has the job of announcing the jury vote and the people's vote in a lively and interesting way without holding up the proceedings. And then the scoreboard has got to work.

"This year's theme is diversity. Let's see who they've chosen to host. Oh, it's three white men."

Graham Norton

GREEN ROOM MOMENTS TO CHERISH

To give the organizers time to reset the stage, one of the presenters is detailed to mingle with the contestants once they have performed. This presenter has to wander the huge open space where each country's team is gathered in a couch cluster with flags, mascots, and bottles of champagne, and ask them how they feel. We have listened to several hours of Green Room reactions, so you don't have to.

" We werry werry happy in Belarus. "

MY EMOTIONS, VERY VERY MUCH!

I HAD THE TIME OF MY LIFE.

I FELT A BIG WAVE IN MY BODY.

AMAZING, I AM VERY, VERY HAPPY. I CAN'T
REMEMBER EVERYTHING WHEN I GO ON STAGE,
I FELT GREAT.

MY LUCKY CHARM IS MY HAT.

MY PERFORMANCE IS FROM THE HEART.

AMAZING! WHEN I GOT ON STAGE THIS IS MY
MOMENT. MY BEST PERFORMANCE EVER.

WE FINALLY LEARNT TO WALK WITH THE DRESSES.

I DREW ON MY BELLY "I LOVE YOU MUM."

MY LUCK IS I BELIEVE IN GOD.

FEELS GOOD TO BE WHERE WE ARE.

CROWD WAS AMAZING.

IT WAS FABULOUS! SO FUN, CHAMPAGNE!

THREE MINUTES FULL OF ENERGY, CROWD
WAS WITH YOU, HEY.

I'VE GOT MY LUCKY SOCKS ON.

THE BEST TIME! OVER TOO SOON—I WISH
I COULD HAVE STOPPED TIME.

FIRST TIME I FELT SO MANY PEOPLE WATCHING
AND SUPPORTING. I HAD GREAT EMOTIONS.

"The Norwegian commentator sees his role as "not being mean to anyone as they are all doing their best." Did you hear that, Graham? "

THE PRESENTERS

Chosen by the host National Broadcaster, the presenters are a vital part of the live show. The memorable faces of Eurovision from way back when it all began, are **Corry Brokken** the Dutch singer who represented her country three years in a row, then returned to host in 1976, and Britain's **Katie Boyle**, a legend in Eurovision's lifetime, presenting the show an unprecedented four times with elegance, charm, and some lovely frocks.

In no particular order, here are some of the other standouts from the past 65 years:

Lill Lindfors, Swedish stand-up comedian and singer who competed in 1966 (coming second) and brought genuine joy and laughter to the 1985 contest. Memorable for a staged wardrobe malfunction when she appeared to have torn her dress and exposed her underwear, but a cunning tug on the Velcro® revealed a whole new look. Nice One!

Anke Engelke, German comedian who shone as part of a three-way hosting gig in 2011. Witty and professional, she is also the German voice of Marge Simpson. In 2012 she was called upon to present the German voting scores when the contest was held in Baku, Azerbaijan. She prefaced her announcement with a statement about human rights in that country, the only person in the room to acknowledge the elephant.

Assi Azar, was part of the four-man hosting team for Israel in 2019. He saw off the other three with his goofy antics and energetic enthusiasm. Went a bit crazy on stage and in the Green Room and everyone loved him to bits. Built a career on it.

Mikko Leppilampi, Finnish actor and musician, was chosen to host the 2007 competition after Lordi won for Finland for the first and only time the previous year. He had charm, he had charisma, he had confidence, and was voted among the best presenters ever. He is regarded as the most promising star of Finland's movie industry. That's what Eurovision can do for a career.

Erik Solbakken presented for Norway in 2010. He was fun! He sang and danced! He ripped off his clothes to reveal a green leotard and got down with the contestants in the Green Room! You've got to make an impact.

★ ★ ★

Conchita Wurst. Ahh, the legendary Conchita who caused homophobic Russians to have conniptions when she won in 2014 and became a superstar and Gay Pride icon. She hosted for Austria the following year. Classy, elegant, and funny, she stood up for the poor Russian contestant Polina Gagarina, when she was roundly booed by the audience just for being Russian.

★ ★ ★

Filomena Cautela hosted for Portugal in 2018, along with three other women, but her star shone the brightest. Her job was patrolling the Green Room and, despite English not being her best language, she took to the task with sass and a bit of sarcasm, injecting a definite edge into the usual gush. She's been voted in the top three of all Eurovision presenters. They do like their competitions, these Eurovisioners.

★ ★ ★

Måns Zerlmerlöw, Swedish singer and all-round talented person, won the contest for Sweden in 2015 with "Heroes," and then got to co-host in 2016. Determined to make a difference, he learned a Riverdance routine to liven up the interval acts, and so popular was he that he was asked to make a "How to Be a Better Presenter" video which is an industry classic. He's been a part of every Eurovision contest since, performing in the interval. Keep an eye out for him in Turin in 2022.

Petra Mede, Swedish comedian, dancer, and actress who hosted solo in 2013 and co-hosted in 2016 with the lovely Mans (see above). They made the interval acts quite special, became a "dream team" and made a few risky references to the Official Eurovision tat on sale. Sweden haven't won since.

WHO IS IN THE COMMENTARY BOX?

Luckily for the UK we first had **Terry Wogan**, and for the past 12 years **Graham Norton**, who brought their wit and sense of the ridiculous to this frankly bizarre contest, making it a legitimate theatre of the absurd to be celebrated at many different levels.

Other commentators in other countries take the job more seriously. The Spanish have a serious male/light-hearted woman combo who genuinely try to be helpful. The Austrian commentator admits to "teasing a little bit," the Czech takes on the job as if he were a sports commentator and the Dutch guy admits to "a slight sense of irony" but he reins himself in as the Dutch don't go for irony or sarcasm, apparently. Nor do the Norwegians—their commentator sees his role as being supportive and "not being mean to anyone as they are all doing their best." In this book we are firmly on the side of irony and sarcasm.

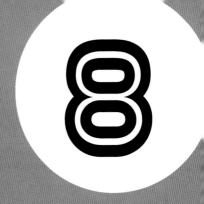

8

WATCH PARTY!

THE MOMENT YOU HAVE ALL BEEN WAITING FOR

There will be competition. One superfan who has been holding parties for 20 years delights his guests with score sheets, themed food and drink, a lighting system, a sound system, and a smoke machine. He also does helium-filled balloons, cake, and themed outfits. The parties are his way of encouraging the spirit of togetherness that Eurovision represents. "The politicians argue about this, that, and the other," he says, "we argue about a song." That's the spirit!

Pity the overseas fans, keen to watch the show live. Devotees in Australia drag themselves out of bed at 4 am, switch on, party up, and breakfast on sausages on sticks and hard liquor. In the USA, as elsewhere, Eurovision is very popular with the gay community, and do they know how to party—imagine clubs and bars at lunchtime, rammed with fans dancing and singing along to bubblegum pop music and wailing anthems. Join in!

GETTING STARTED

Perfect parties need planning. You will need a checklist.

DECORATIONS

You can buy 28-European-Nations flag bunting which may or may not cover all possible 26 finalists. Small flags to dot about the place would be good and little paper flags to stick in the canapés are a nice touch. Balloons, perhaps in the color of the host nation's flag? In 2022 it will be Italy so red, white, and green, bunched together in threes and tied with matching ribbon. Also available from sites that specialize in this kind of thing are Eurovision bedspreads, which make good tablecloths, and Eurovision throws, just the thing for protecting your furniture.

OUTFITS

National costumes should really be discouraged. So often people equate Eurovision dress code with *lederhosen* (uncomfortable, impractical, and very expensive), Tyrolean hats, blonde wigs with plaits, and frocks with aprons. Most European countries have regional national outfits, but it is hard to distinguish a Basque from a Hungarian from a Sardinian, and anyway Britain presents a problem unless you count Wales's tall hats and Scotland's kilts.

Pick a theme. Sparkly spandex? Wrapped in a flag? Everyone knit a Conchita Wurst beard? Heavy metal Lordi horror? Cone hats everyone? Abba tribute? Silver hot pants? There's plenty to choose from in the archive.

If you want to make your party truly memorable, you must think outside the box and Be Different! Go out on a limb and insist everyone comes dressed as a fruit—there are some amazingly gorgeous outfits out there: pineapple and strawberry costumes accompanied by a banana, a slice of lemon, watermelon, and a giant blueberry. Reach into the vegetable box for a red hot chili pepper, a pumpkin, and a carrot. A room full of hysterical Eurovision fruit and veg should make for some memorable Instagram moments.

FOOD

You would go mad producing food from all 26 finalist nations. Go for the Big Five, which in 2022 includes the host nation, Italy, then add something Baltic, something Nordic, and something a bit more exotic from further east.

ITALY

Easiest would be bread sticks wrapped in Parma ham; more impressive are Caprese skewers, for which you need small wooden skewers, little mozzarella balls, cherry tomatoes, and fresh basil leaves. Assemble and drizzle with balsamic condiment. *Perfetto*!

UNITED KINGDOM

Go for something essentially British in the form of ready-made sausage rolls. Serve warm with mustard and plenty of parsley. Perfect!

GERMANY

It's got to be a *Käse Igel*, or Cheese Hedgehog,
a staple German party food. And *sooo* Eurovision.
You will need toothpicks, a selection of German
cheeses such as Emmentaler, Butterkäse, and Tilsit,
some seedless grapes, and half a melon. Cut the
cheeses into cubes, skewer one cube along with a
grape, and stick the picks into the round side of the
melon. *Perfekt!*

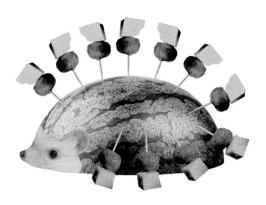

WATCH PARTY!

"Eurovision bedspreads make good tablecloths, and Eurovision throws—just the thing for protecting your furniture. "

SPAIN

An obvious choice is the staple of all tapas bars, a Spanish omelet. You could go and buy one, but sometimes you have to make a bit of an effort. This is a dish to make in advance and serve at room temperature, cut up into squares, skewered with a Spanish flag. For six eggs (scale up as you wish), peel and slice one biggish potato and one large onion. Slices should be thinnish and even, so they cook at the same time. Have ready a sieve set over a bowl, a slotted spoon, another bowl, and a flat plate. Heat a good measure of olive oil in an omelet pan, slide in a layer of sliced onion, followed by a layer of sliced potato, and another layer of onions, and top with potatoes. Season liberally with salt, pepper, and a few flakes of chili and cook gently. The potatoes and onions should be poaching in the oil, not frying. Meanwhile beat the eggs in the bowl, which should be big enough to take the potatoes and onions as well. When the onions and potatoes are soft but not brown (about

20 minutes) scoop them gently out of the pan into the sieve set over a bowl, so the oil drips off. Tip the potato/onion mix into the egg bowl and stir gently to introduce the eggs to the veg. Leave them to mingle for about 10 minutes. Attend now to your omelet pan: if there's a lot of oil, pour some off and keep it. Pour the egg mix into the pan and cook gently, shaking it about a bit to get the runny bits to the bottom. When it looks set enough to turn over, slide it out on to the plate and, adding some more oil if necessary, flip it back into the pan with the uncooked side downward. Do not overcook! As soon as it stops being runny in the middle, turn it out and let it cool. Sprinkle everything with parsley. *Perfeta!*

FRANCE

Prepare a generous platter of *charcuterie* for your guests. Bear in mind France has won the competition five times, come second five times, and third seven times, so they are a force to be reckoned with and need to be well represented. You will need:

A SELECTION OF HAMS:
cooked ham, cured ham such as Bayonne ham,
a *jambon sec* like the hams from the Ardèche.
SALAMIS:
rosette, *saucisson de Lyons*, and *saucisson d'Arles*,
par example.
PÂTÉS:
coarse pork pâté, smooth duck or chicken liver,
and delicious rabbit pâté if you can find it.
Consider also spreadables, like *rillettes*.
CHEESES:
one soft cheese, one hard, one goat, and one blue.
That should do it.
SOMETHING SWEET:
fresh and dried fruits like grapes, figs, cherry tomatoes,
and fruity chutneys.
SOMETHING SALTY:
olives, salted nuts, tapenade.
SOMETHING CRUNCHY:
cornichons, radishes, celery, fennel.
BREAD:
sourdough and a baguette.

Assemble artistically and sprinkle with rocket. *Parfait*!

SOMETHING BALTIC

Pickles are hugely popular in this region. They are a bit tedious to make yourself, so go shopping and stock up on pickled cabbage, cucumbers, onions, carrots, and beetroot and serve up with rye bread. *Täiuslik*!

SOMETHING NORDIC

It should really be something to do with herring, but that's not really finger food. How about little blinis, spread generously with sour cream, a bit of smoked salmon, half a teaspoonful of lumpfish caviar, a grind of black pepper, a squish of lemon, decorated with a tiny sprig of dill. *Täydellinen*! (that's Finnish)

SOMETHING EXOTIC

You can buy a tub of *baba ganoush*, an eggplant (aubergine) dip, but it is easy to make yourself. Scoop the flesh from two large eggplants (aubergines) that you have baked in the oven until floppy and blackened, add a couple of tablespoons of tahini, four tablespoons of Greek yogurt, the juice of two lemons, a crushed clove of garlic, and some salt. Mix up, add a chopped chili if you like, decant into a pretty bowl and scatter some pomegranate seeds on the top. Serve with strips of flatbread. *Orexi*! (that's Greek)

Harry Craddock, legendary barman at the Savoy Hotel back in the 1930s, was once asked the best way to drink a cocktail:

"Quickly," replied the great man, "while it's laughing at you!"

DRINK

It's going to be a long night, so start with a stock of soft drinks in rainbow colors, served in colored plastic tumblers with paper straws. Leave good taste in the closet in the hall, to be picked up as your guests leave the premises. Old-fashioned cordials come in interesting shades. Dandelion and Burdock, Sarsparilla, and Blackcurrant and Liquorice are dark and dangerous looking. Rhubarb, Cranberry, and Pomegranate a zingy red, while Ginger, Gooseberry, and Elderflower run the gamut from yellow to green. The joy of a decent cordial is that you can slosh some vodka into it when necessary.

Cocktails are mandatory. Especially cocktails that no one drinks any more because they are no longer fashionable. Shake or stir the following.

APEROL SPRITZ

You'll need a long glass for this one. It could take a parasol and a wedge of orange.

1¼oz (35ml) Aperol
2oz (60ml) Prosecco
splash of soda water
wedge of orange, for garnish

No shaker required for this one. Simply place the ice in the glass, pour over the Aperol and the Prosecco, splash in soda water to taste, garnish, and serve.

PINA COLADA

Tall glass and a blender required.

4oz (120ml) pineapple juice
2oz (60ml) white rum
2oz (60ml) coconut cream
wedge of pineapple, and a cocktail cherry, for garnish

Pulse the pineapple juice, rum, and coconut cream along with a handful of ice in a blender until smooth. Pour into a tall glass and garnish.

WATCH PARTY!

TEQUILA SUNRISE

A long glass, a cherry on a stick, and a paper parasol are required for this. What's not to love?

2 tsp Grenadine
ice
1¾oz (50ml) tequila
1 tbsp triple sec
1 large orange, or 2 small ones, juiced
½ lemon, juiced
1 cocktail cherry, for garnish

Pour the grenadine into the bottom of a tall glass and set aside. Fill a cocktail shaker with ice and add the tequila, triple sec, and orange and lemon juices. Shake until the outside of the shaker feels icy to the touch. Add a few ice cubes to the glass then carefully strain the cocktail into it, trying not to disturb the grenadine layer too much. Add more ice as needed to fill the glass, then garnish your sunrise with the parasol and cocktail cherry.

CLASSIC COSMOPOLITAN

The Cosmopolitan may be pink and passé, but come on, it's Eurovision!

1½oz (45ml) vodka
¾oz (20ml) Cointreau or triple sec
½oz (15ml) cranberry juice
splash of freshly squeezed lime juice
ice
lime slice, for garnish

Place a martini glass in the freezer to chill. Combine the vodka, Cointreau or triple sec, cranberry juice, and lime juice in a cocktail shaker and fill it halfway with ice. Shake vigorously until the outside of the shaker is icy to the touch. Strain into the chilled glass and garnish.

CODA

There has been a movie made about Eurovision, *The Story of Fire Saga*. At the time of writing it was getting great reviews and was number one on Netflix's most-watched chart. It is an affectionate comedy (what else) that follows the fortunes of Fire Saga, an Icelandic band selected to perform for their country at the Eurovision Song Contest. It is packed with references that will delight Eurovision fans. There's a band called Moon Fang, unashamedly channeling Eurovision winners Lordi, down to their horror masks and leather trousers, and there are performances from real-life contestants Alexander Rybak, Conchita Wurst, and Netta. The phenomenon that is Eurovision just grows and grows. Enjoy!

EUROVISION WINNERS

YEAR	COUNTRY	PERFORMER(S)	SONG
1956	Switzerland	**Lys Assia**	"Refrain"
1957	Netherlands	**Corry Brokken**	"Net Als Toen"
1958	France	**André Claveau**	"Dors, Mon Amour"
1959	Netherlands	**Teddy Scholten**	"Een Beetje"
1960	France	**Jacqueline Boyer**	"Tom Pillibi"
1961	Luxembourg	**Jean-Claude Pascal**	"Nous Les Amoureux"
1962	France	**Isabelle Aubret**	"Un Premier Amour"
1963	Denmark	**Grethe & Jørgen Ingmann**	"Dansevise"
1964	Italy	**Gigliola Cinquetti**	"Non Ho L'Eta"
1965	Luxembourg	**France Gall**	"Poupée De Cire, Poupée De Son"
1966	Austria	**Udo Jürgens**	"Merci, Chérie"
1967	UK	**Sandie Shaw**	"Puppet On A String"
1968	Spain	**Massiel**	"La La La"
1969	Spain	**Salomé**	"Vivo Cantando"
1969	UK	**Lulu**	"Boom Bang-A-Bang"
1969	Netherlands	**Lenny Kuhr**	"De Troubadour"
1969	France	**Frida Boccara**	"Un Jour, Un Enfant"
1970	Ireland	**Dana**	"All Kinds Of Everything"
1971	Monaco	**Séverine**	"Un Banc, Un Arbre, Une Rue"
1972	Luxembourg	**Vicky Leandros**	"Après Toi"
1973	Luxembourg	**Anne-Marie David**	"Tu Te Reconnaîtras"
1974	Sweden	**ABBA**	"Waterloo"
1975	Netherlands	**Teach-In**	"Ding-A-Dong"
1976	UK	**Brotherhood of Man**	"Save Your Kisses For Me"
1977	France	**Marie Myriam**	"L'Oiseau Et L'Enfant"
1978	Israel	**Izhar Cohen & Alphabeta**	"A-Ba-Ni-Bi"
1979	Israel	**Milk and Honey**	"Hallelujah"
1980	Ireland	**Johnny Logan**	"What's Another Year?"
1981	UK	**Bucks Fizz**	"Making Your Mind Up"
1982	Germany	**Nicole**	"Bin Bisschen Frieden"
1983	Luxembourg	**Corinne Hermès**	"Si La Vie Est Cadeau"
1984	Sweden	**Herreys**	"Diggi-Loo Diggi-Ley"
1985	Norway	**Bobbysocks!**	"La Det Swinge"
1986	Belgium	**Sandra Kim**	"J'aime La Vie"
1987	Ireland	**Johnny Logan**	"Hold Me Now"
1988	Switzerland	**Celine Dion**	"Ne Partez Pas Sans Moi"
1989	Yugoslavia	**Riva**	"Rock Me"
1990	Italy	**Toto Cutugno**	"Insieme: 1992"
1991	Sweden	**Carola**	"Fångad Av En Stormvind"

YEAR	COUNTRY	PERFORMER(S)	SONG
1992	Ireland	**Linda Martin**	"Why Me?"
1993	Ireland	**Niamh Kavanagh**	"In Your Eyes"
1994	Ireland	**Paul Harrington with Charlie McGettigan**	"Rock 'n' Roll Kids"
1995	Norway	**Secret Garden**	"Nocturne"
1996	Ireland	**Eimear Quinn**	"The Voice"
1997	UK	**Katrina and the Waves**	"Love Shine A Light"
1998	Israel	**Dana International**	"Diva"
1999	Sweden	**Charlotte Nilsson**	"Take Me To Your Heaven"
2000	Denmark	**Olsen Brothers**	"Fly On The Wings of Love"
2001	Estonia	**Tanel Padar, Dave Benton, and 2XL**	"Everybody"
2002	Latvia	**Marie N**	"I Wanna"
2003	Turkey	**Sertab Erener**	"Every Way That I Can"
2004	Ukraine	**Ruslana**	"Wild Dances"
2005	Greece	**Helena Paparizou**	"My Number One"
2006	Finland	**Lordi**	"Hard Rock Hallelujah"
2007	Serbia	**Marija Šerifović**	"Molitva"
2008	Russia	**Dima Bilan**	"Believe"
2009	Norway	**Alexander Rybak**	"Fairy Tale"
2010	Germany	**Lena**	"Satellite"
2011	Azerbaijan	**Ell & Nikki**	"Running Scared'
2012	Sweden	**Loreen**	"Euphoria"
2013	Denmark	**Emmelie de Forest**	"Only Teardrops"
2014	Austria	**Conchita Wurst**	"Rise Like A Phoenix"
2015	Sweden	**Måns Zelmerlöw**	"Heroes"
2016	Ukraine	**Jamala**	"1944"
2017	Portugal	**Salvador Sobral**	"Amar Pelos Dois"
2019	Netherlands	**Duncan Laurence**	"Arcade"
2021	Italy	**Måneskin**	"Zitti E Buoni"

ACKNOWLEDGEMENTS

My thanks to Penny Craig, Sally Powell, Blair Frame, and Louise Leffler, for joining the crazy ride that is Eurovision with such enthusiasm and talent.

143

INDEX